MORNING PRAYER

בס"ד

for Rabbi Silber,

with much admiration
and gratitude,

Eve 12·13·05

MORNING PRAYER

POEMS

EVE GRUBIN

THE SHEEP MEADOW PRESS
RIVERDALE-ON-HUDSON, NY

All inquiries and permission requests should be addressed to:
The Sheep Meadow Press
P.O. Box 1345
Riverdale-on-Hudson, NY 10471

Designed and typeset by The Sheep Meadow Press.
Distributed by The University Press of New England.

Printed on acid-free paper in the United States. This book meets the guidelines
for permanence and durability of the Committee on
Production Guidelines for Book Longevity of the Council on Library
Resources.

Library of Congress Cataloging-in-Publication Data

Grubin, Eve.
Morning prayer / Eve Grubin.
p. cm.
Includes bibliographical references.
ISBN 1-931357-28-5 (alk. paper)
I. Title.

PS3607.R685M67 2005
811'.6--dc22

2005027590

CONTENTS

MORNING PRAYER

AFTER

After a loss you live
with your gasp, your gaze,

with your hungry mouth as you lift the fork.

Something Sane. Open the door.
A guest sits down at the kitchen table.

Washing evening dishes:
something simple, something sane.
Water dreams over your wrist,
your hand, a round
transparent dish.

Something Simple. Night, rusty fire escape.
Even the rain: sane.

Urgent street voices; screech
of a hinge. *Simple.* A clanking
bang,

somebody is closing a gate
or opening one.

I

YOU BREATHED IT INTO ME

I fail. Every morning shade drawn,
hair brushed, swaying, I can't

fasten to the words, Hebrew letters
breathe, young sparrows in my palm.

Yes, calm stands up in the coolness
of morning, light pushes, falls

from under the shade's edges.
A skittering stops me at each syllable. I turn,

check my hair in the mirror, the line of my skirt,
picture someone watching. I imagine being

observed by an admirer, my mind
startles from words my tongue makes

in the four minutes I give
each morning to speak to no human.

RELIGION

The wingbeat of the flock would not lift.
Sadness kept bringing more feathers
until the day itself was sad.

In the dream I heard,
There is Father in the signs of breaking up.

What I slept was shed.
What I could not sleep, I wept.

The wings were hands heavy in their bones,
a hard flutter beating gray.
The hands: slow, wet and down-turned.

I slept through the losses, through
the years, slept the wingbeat and the tears,
the flock, sometimes soft and red, the bones.

In the dream the rabbi said,
The food you are eating does not nourish you.

How to push out the wings without tearing?

On the Sabbath I stop. The wings still.
The blessed food nourishes.
A wild calm springs from this new sanity.

In the dream the rabbi's modesty made him turn away
when he saw me standing alone by the water
in my bathing suit.
He simply went, walked home through the wet reeds.

What I slept was shed.
What I could not sleep, I wept.
What I could not write, I prayed.

MORNING PRAYER

It's not the prayer. It's the preparation for prayer.

Less the body than voice, breath, gaze.

It's not faith, it's faltering.

Less happiness than the laws.
It's not survival.

It's the battle, desire and modesty, the name. Near.
Not near; awe.

Clothing on the body. Distinguishing between night and
waking.

Not ambition; silence. Not silence; family.
Not your loving; self.

Not *in* peace; *toward* peace.

Less the individual than the group. It's a single human life.

Less the prayer than the story. Less the story than
the story underneath the story.

Not kindness; un-hatred.
Not the Nazi, but the Angel of Death.

Not nature but history. Not region;
time. Not human; gender. It's human.

Less asking than gratitude. Less grieving than
praise. It's grieving and praise.

Not sex, but two souls. Not ashes;
the body. Less the body than dust.

Trampling, gold song. Pining, scent, shelter. It's not
the preparation for prayer. It's the morning.

THE BURIED RIB CAGE

Eve slipped from its arced ridge—
the only body part
you don't
             do evil with:

the eye, the hand,
might beg
                corruption;

the ribs are modest
shy crests, ticklish,
                        an open fan,
not quite sexual, yet not puritan:

delicate accordion
                        —yawn, moan—
soul breathes through its comb.

10

HOW THE RAIN

When it began to come down hard
we were thankful. We had lived

the long barren breaths without jagged edges,
we had spoken
the guttural letters forgetting desire's torn robe.

Belief had us blindfolded.
Dead grass, numb wholeness, too complete, as if
done.

We let the rain fill us, breaking into
our soft shoulders, the wrinkles in our psalms,

pulsing the new chords we had failed
to hear in our own holy texts.

We turned our hands over, the rush
drenching our knuckles, filling

the white spaces in our untouched scrolls.

Ink spread and ran into our shoes, into our black coats and hair,
slackening the blind's blue bind.

Opening our mouths to broken points
bright pinpricks hit our tongues and lips.

It kept coming, kept weaving
through us until we stopped

having faith so we could doubt
again, believe.

BELIEF

A light was planted in the world.
I sleep tangled

in white sheets
or eat with a spoon half-listening

to the radio.
The planted light grew into morning.

Sometimes with my back on the earth
history folds.

The grass is dry, the garden untended.
On the bottom of the pool, mud.

Now tangled, now planted, the light
is physical. It was *made.*

HAND IS A METAPHOR

First the laws, the unseen foundations.
Then: water, snow–light, silt.

All matter is based on the initial guidelines.
As you read this, rules breathe through the macadam.

Hand is a metaphor for the original *hand*. And a tree
represents the *tree*. Even the essence of *eating*
signifies the forgotten thing.

Numinous is not the right word.
It's more like praise or *inexplicable
suffering* or...

I want to know: what was *human*?

Walking under streetlamps or along rocky
winter roads
it is not possible
to remember shades behind,
the laws before although

there is a stickiness
between past and opaque present.

The laws are a channel.

What was *human*?

The laws are a channel.
A space for God to swim.

UNHAPPINESS ON EARTH

Even now I may not be

speaking from myself but from some character in whose soul
I now live.

I am certain. I have not one idea of the truth
of any of my speculations. Heaven is like unhappiness

on earth only inverted into a finer tone.
I am certain of nothing.

Call the world, if you please, *the vale of soul making*
then you will find out the use of the world.

I am certain of nothing but the holiness.
Do you see how necessary a world of pain is?

I am certain of nothing but the holiness of the heart's affections and
the truth of imagination.

I was led into these thoughts by the beauty
of the morning operating on a sense of idleness.

I am certain of nothing but and.

I have not understood any books.
The morning said I was right.

MESSIAH

When buildings are lamps oceans ink

and all the gathered waters

when the winds are hands when the sands are canvas

and all the stones and ash

form the first shapes of language

the original shades

I'll provide an unthreaded cloak

a clear screen to look through

I'll bring you inside the gesture

to the shadow beside each illness each pain

I'll bear a sheet of water

when the sun falls into the water

we will shed the old hopes

walk through the sun's pupil

step into—

SEDUCTION

A sea change is necessary, and I'll need seduction,
a tug through language in my belly's earth floor.

★

God planted
a garden in Eden to the East
and took and placed
the person there.

The questions are asked: "Where was Adam taken from?
How did God bring Adam to Eden? Was Adam moved
like a chess piece?"

An answer: "God moved, seduced Adam with beautiful
language into Eden."

★

Word-shiver my shells, my salt
nearer to you.

★

I am a salamander frail and pale red, and you
place rich leaves and pebbles before me, drawing

my tender same-color feet to touch
each dry curve, scratch the wrinkled places, your sounds

of wind and rumpled lake, scrape of dry twigs.
Speak speak to me.

Evoke yourself in me. Blossom my chest open with text,
with words.

JERUSALEM

In the dream I walk with my teacher across a field.
It is day, the field
a dying brown.
Lifted by sudden wind we stand
in midair, our wool coats hanging
like heavy curtains.

When we drop back down, our boots in the dust,
I ask, "Why did that happen?"
She says, "Because we saw Christ."
I say, "I didn't see him," remembering
the sycamores at the edges.
She says, "It was because of the resurrection."
"No," I say. "It was Jerusalem."

Keep me close to the flaw,
to the cracked soil. Don't let me
fly up again; keep me living
inside the laws and the lightning, planted
and learning, leaning
into this difficult field.

II

A CLEFT

A cleft in the light.

Did the winds from the blackbirds disturb
the window?

I was aware of matches
struck and storms. Word storms.

It wasn't sexual night. It wasn't waking
from a dream. It was something else entirely.

Signs on trains moved, and voices
clouded forward.
Dead words. Not the ones we heard

when we marched on Washington.
Heels clicked, clefs of sound.
Glass and dry leaves in the sounds.

They were taking me to St. Barnabas,
I kept saying, *Burn the bus!*

My daughter. I lost. Her little fingers
warm as August wind, her eyes.

Everything gone. Husband, ring, mother-
in-law, Europe where he treated me like a queen.

When they gave me drugs, in the light:
a permanent cleft. Dry sand splitting

the Red Sea.
My daughter wrote this poem.
Not night. Not me.

HINGE

When the hinge in my mother's mind split

loose rust

came down like pollen onto my eyelids, my lips.

Doors no longer flapped open, shut.
They hung.
The rust kissed my knees, the bend
of my arm.

On the brass hinge: nesting starlings,
spiders shaping wet webs.

Shavings from felled trees among the daddy longlegs.

I put gauze over the rust as if it were blood.
As if it were my
crushed hinge that stippled the pine floor red.

MOTHER AND CHILD

She kneeled at the hill's base, stirred
the new season,

held the scent of cut lawn in her palms.

Sprinklers arched into spring with a confident grace
I have not seen since.

The water flecks swept, lingered
like the stretching arms of a waking woman.

Her arms covered and honest, open to receive
my tangled hair, white pants, grass-stained at the knees.
I am afraid

of this distinct joy, scared to praise.
She smiled with a sensible pleasure

I have not seen since.

Running down that hill I let... I
let the urgent wind bite through my open jacket and T-shirt.

Pay attention, it's hard to admit:
I offered my body to it.

RUINS

My bike became a horse
pitching me off
onto the steep, unforgiving concrete,

sudden and alone, small stones pressed into my cheek,
the rubber wheels hot horse hooves. Earth pulse
through my skin. Black descending dust.

In the small space between tears I saw
my sanity: blue lights among timber, broken marble,
calm resting in ruins, light playing
among the jagged remains.

When I arrived back again,
the voiceless horse became the bike's thin singing metal
and myself, resting in the wreck.

THE MOTHER

A sudden noise stood
in my shoes.

The other children fix
my daughter's hair, with bows
and barrettes and combing.
They know how to be
with her, she cries when I
arrive.

Cold water up to my ankles, and
ice in my shoes, the voice
rises from there,
through my thighs and eyes,
stands in my hands.

We lit the little braided Channukah candle.
Amen, she sang. A man.
He is leaving
his ring in the kitchen garbage, the ice
is breaking my knees.

PRESENCE

Her presence: a thin shadow along the seam of my robe.

She gave me a small oak box with a story
painted on the lid.
Blanched wood shines through the cracked paint.

BROOKLYN WINDOW

In the photograph the gaps in her smoke-black hair—

the thin, bare, scared places,
between the strands of silky soot: invisible tears.

Morning pulses through the Brooklyn window, an unmourned
morning,

pounding blue fire widening through the translucency

of her round red shirt, her face modest, a shyness
around her mouth

and her breast a red shadow;

her scent changing color in the deepening humble light
is the deepening humble light.

The newspaper's pages unwrap, pages turning
into a new hope—1969, 1970—marching
brave toward an unknown integrity,

an unraveling of the old scent, her beauty
is exactly right as

an ash in her mind detaches, one thought

uncoupled from the next
thought and the next one charred, exhausted.

Soon I will cry out,
be born

to the books on the windowsill, to the dust.

The tears alive, black fire on white fire

and in the spaces between
her red shirt and
my scent.

SANITY

Lips part like curtains   hair loosens

           ★

Supple as the bridge's frame is soft   built to bend

           ★

When the mother restrains a wrestling child
she grips the child close

to stop a fall   still

she allows
a softness in her limbs

REFUSAL

There is a refusal to mourn
in me, a failure
to give up hope, a rotting
thing, no
thing. Nothing.

There is a river. I'll dip
my hands in, open
my fingers.

I never mourned, never
allowed a falling

the way divine sparks slanted
when the world was made dipping
under rocks, resting in meadows and seas, leaning
among fish, grasses, and dust.

Is mourning a handing over,
a letting go of the steel grip? How to ungrasp
like the trapeze artist who opens her hand,
letting go the bar
before grasping the other—that moment between the bars....

Let me rise like a great white bird out of the net, let me
climb into the underwhisper.

I have had moments that make hope
superfluous.

There is a river. I have never
seen it.

WHO HAS PROVIDED ME MY EVERY NEED

Even after starved sleep.

Even when waiting in shadow
for the Wednesday train,

even when standing in the center of the oar-deep week,

when morning lays its arm on the sidewalk
the blue presses from underneath, *sanity*.

Even in sunup's lean light.
Even before bread
and fruit, even with the veil laid over the day.

Looking back, Monday and Tuesday are twins,
my shoes pressing like reality
against the subway platform's coarse pavement.

Even in a crowd, even with the
gloom through my shirt—sleeved, faithful.

Even as the train howls toward us,
men and women gazing out
or staring.

Even as I join them.
They glance and watch in cars of light.

THE SANE MOTHER

A woman attaches a sheet to the clothesline
with a wooden pin, her hair a loose
knot at the back of her neck; she pauses
to handle the cotton between her fingers.
Morning. Days are long.
Every day
she places the empty
basket on the kitchen table, dries her hands
on the red dish towel.
The radio is a brook trembling
over toothed stones.
The city is far. Every day
reaching for the sponge,
she closes her eyes, listens
for the breathing of children
who lie uncovered upstairs.
Maybe this is what sanity looks like:
raw grass blades wet on the soles
of her feet, arms to elbows in soapy water,
she lifts a glass to the light—broken
points of blue pass through—
lowers it to her other hand, begins
to wash it.

THE GIRL'S DREAM

In the beginning: the original pain,

unremembered by the girl,
though her body held it tight,
secure so as not to lose
the shame

which was the second pain:
the father who turned from her.

The girl's dream sought to curve against him:
the father's eyes are open

behind round glasses, listening to her hurt
in the daylight.

Back in the outer world, the father continued
to be the father,
and there was the first pain
and the second.

MY FATHER'S WORDS

When my father said it
the room tilted,

our bodies tipped
left on the angle with sloping floors and walls.

His words formed a single sob
blossoming above my tongue,
the sob rose as my arms reached out

for balance, my hands touched his soft
shirt in a gesture
to push him from the room.

Seduced by an image of himself as gentle, my father
looked surprised when

the words coming out of his mouth stopped.
Everything outside—car alarms,

voices in the courtyard—went
silent. Just me and my father locked

in the infinite
quilted quiet of the room. And suspended

above our heads—grotesque
stars on a moonless night—his curse and my sob.

THINK OF THIS

1

Once there was a ripping.

It was like a gash
on the breast.
Not along the seam. A cleaving
at an impossible place in the middle.

A ripping. And the child emerged
from the unfeasible,
crawled through slats of light streaked
across each wall, each closed door.

The child stopped in a room that seemed to explain.
She stood up, stepped
into the room's wound:

wrought-iron gates, muddy bodies, dreams
of throats convulsing.

Unseamed explanations, a dangerous peace.
She lay down.

2

The women gather around the burnt-out fire.
Smoke rising from the center, a black braid.

Seven in white nightgowns float in the brown fields.
Wrens and marigolds embroidered on the cotton sleeves
loose around their wrists.

In the forest the child stumbles near
a woman with unraveling green stems in her fist who is unaware
of the long scratch on her own face,

a shaft of light hits the pine-needle floor beside them.

                         3
Can you think of this as an instruction,
a preparation?

This cutting
to the sap
and knurl, this clawing to the root?

A severe angel catches
                         your wrist:

This obstruction
is a preparation and an entrance.

You will be a woman
such as makes others glad to be born.

                         4
Sanity's sand is soaked, dark.

Its plum is cold.

And its lines are the perfect black blurs
on the bottom of the swimming pool.

Taste it: faint tang of chlorine
when you lick your knee.

5

Sanity knows a body enters another body as a dream
enters the next dream,

knows about sorrow's orb, an odor
carried in a net.

The burnt hour slights the father's obstructing words.
Brush the words away, they are flies circling a summer face.

Across the surface of the earth
hurt lies lustrous.

JERUSALEM II

Unmoving on the edge
of Israel, on the edge of Palestine,

everything an edge: his empty
lap, the night, my crying like a child
in his motionless car. *I am so hungry.*

    Everyone is.

No, I am the only one...

All edges touching.
Words beating stone, night. Words

dipping into the eye
of the world.

WHAT HAPPENED

I wish I never saw those movies
of blood and rocks of cut screams and unopened hands.

The one with the Australian girls who imagined their own kingdom
and lived in it, who chase the woman through certainty's forest

and beat her with a bag of rocks until her head is blood.
The images of drama do not reveal the essence, the images hide,

just as words create an opaque covering, words telling only
a shaded story. Telling "what happened" isn't what happened;

what happened is remote, impossible, not here, a hurled light.
My story only gets in the way of my story,

gets in the way of your knowing what
happened. I don't know how to tell you this, every word

written is deceit, all these words are getting in the way. Let's look
at the white slivers between the words, not what the letters spell,

rather, what they frame: see the shape inside each letter—the lit tent.
What they spell is the rock, the blinding scream. Where is the story?

In the spaces? Is it breathing there? Asking and giving, living in the gaps?
In the precise imagined hollows?

THE UNKNOWING

When I tell
some look at me, their eyes widen,
they back away, smile
and nod, backing away,

some come close wanting
to hear more, and they step in
and stare the way a man
approaches pornography, his hands
are numb, nothing
can stop him now from his movement
toward a body he will never come
to know.

III

DESIRE

God unpoured the wine out of Eve

to create delay, the gap between wanting
and the wanted.

Before, with the wine pouring through her,
desire for touch blazed simultaneous with touch, flame to flame.

My desire lags, without speech.
Mute, a weight in my eyes, a whistling cavern in my knees.

Your desire will be to your husband and he will rule over you.

God unpoured the wine out of Eve and the birds began yearning.

A woman desires her husband as the rain wants the earth
to need it, as my transgressions hope I will seek them, as God wants
me to pray.

I have been told
that force has no significance. No soul moves by force.

What I want will not come to me just because I desire it.
I have been told that I cannot force.

I don't know how this will end.

God unpoured the wine out of Eve. I don't know the end to this story.

THE NINETEENTH-CENTURY NOVEL

Sometimes I just want to give in, become
the heroine in a great nineteenth-century novel,
an earnest and suffering young woman
who makes the decision that will ruin
the rest of her life.

Once the decision has been made
I want—in my white nightgown—
to unlatch the shutter, throw
open the window,
cry out into the rain.

If not Cathy could I at least be
Elizabeth Bennet living
on the precipice of vast disappointment,
on the edge of loneliness and family shame.
To dip just under the surface of the worst
and then be pulled out
just in time.

THE DATE

Not through a kiss but through his solitary gaze
slanting when I lifted my hair wet-heavy with downpour

heaped it on top of my head elbows pointing neck tilted the meat
restaurant window bleared

with water smeared beaded with dust and haze we talked
Malamud and Rashi and forgiveness

the Jewish way a letting go of blame because we are not the final judge
how it's freeing "liberating" he said his gaze lay

agitated on the bend between my shoulder and chin what is
a single look? what is *seeing*? how it digs hard horse hooves striking

dry ground a smack against your chest stoned
from soup hot in my throat and his eyes

regarding the skin just above my clavicle rain
plunged hard behind his round glasses and black skullcap

pounding the umbrellas and gutters and later
that week my friend told me he'd said to her "I could

tie you to the bed" when I heard that it was as if
I had already heard it soup-heat blushed my tongue his look

searing my collarbone I tell you his eyes flared
as if his troubled intellectual mouth tied me

IN THE GARDEN

Before she met him, she had already met him.
"Look at these flowers," he says.
A motor in wet streets, hands
through rained-on leaves.
Before she met him,
the flowers were already spreading
their petals in her mind.
Words spoken under white,
slow lamp-spots in the room.
Gates clank open, closed.
"These flowers," he says, kissing them.
Dappled moon before him and dappled
moon and snow now, the subway
rolls, rings. Planes arc through thick wind.
Shaded edges of crumpled pillows.
Between his fingers the flowers,
hard stems and petals yellow.
Someone laughs outside.
He held the flowers before
as he holds them now.
Tomatoes, baskets, cobbled road.
Lace hangs along limestone.
Pieces of silver. Near their room,
helicopters across the water.
Pages are tearing.
Steel ropes, an elevator descends, rises.
Lights blink off, buildings pierce clouds.
"Look at these," now whispering.
Jagged roads, mud,
trenched dirt. Shade mingles
among shrubs along a road's edge.
He holds the flowers in his hands.

HIGH SCHOOL

I can't remember if we feared
being seen. Lit doorway,

my right foot in a black heel deep
in the shadowed gap between his shoes.

The pulse from the dance down the block
still vibrating in the soles

of our feet, stockings between my thighs,
his belt buckle brushing against my stomach.

I had never been so inside an autumn night.

New York City gray
flanking the brick building, blown bags
and dry leaves float above the pavement;

a hunger unfastens the catch,
scent of antique wounds released

rising with my arms, arcing around his shoulders
in the glowing **doorway.**

UNREQUITED

1

It was the summer I couldn't get outside.
Even the edges didn't glimmer.

August, Vermont, everything unfurled, loud
fields. Sudden flapping of the river
birds among cattails.

I was aware of squirrels.
They crossed my path, disappeared,
claws clutching the knobby bark.
Clouds moved with a grand
ease behind twisted
ropes of telephone wire,
or was sky moving behind clouds?

There was so much happening:
broken glass around the porch light, slow
crush of gravel, rips in each leaf.
Cobalt sky, heat
rising off tar, eye of a crow.
Rips were far. Not distance-far—

2

Last night, the rabbi: *There is no such thing
as unrequited love.*

Morning radio, hair wet,
dressed but no shoes.
Air conditioning lays its chill
across my unresting arm.
I try to believe.

The future glances inward
breathing the inevitable
across the tiny hairs on my limbs.
The music in the wall's cracks
tries to tell me.
I hear sounds and a few words but not
what is said.

Ruth in the field listened, corn husks in her fists.
On the cool granary floor: wheat, shredded
chaffs, a man.

She is waiting to find out, a voice
reaches out from the threshing floor,
through the husks and wheat.
She uncovers his feet.

3

He touched
my arm across the table in the restaurant.
Not my flesh,
my arm through my sweater.
The soft part, on top, below the elbow.
He touched it with his hand.

I could see him across the table,
looked at him. Kept looking.
He lifted a glass.

And here I am again: the radio
talking, streets talking.
Everything trying to tell me.
The clock and the shadows
and all the books on my bookshelves.

The rabbi said, *Soul knowledge*
is an internal event. Open will.

Give up your want to get what
you wanted. Open

to what you sought without knowing it, to what
you wanted all along.

MARRIAGE DREAM

No picket fence, no jeweled ring or graceful
kitchen. Just me standing on the blond floorboards

in my white nightgown. Wind lifted
the curtains just barely. Intermittent radio sounds

sprinkling through the window gave
depth to the quiet.

As the silence widened
flowers unlocked thick hearts, powdery faces reaching,

fireworks released,
each color a thumbprint expanding,

contracting, powder festooned
the floor with its reds and blues, spores across a yellow dome.

A smile broke, hallowed, calm; not a laugh but a grin, noiseless.
My legs becoming the urgent radio voices

now collecting themselves,
invisible silver slivers pointed through my chest and my hair.

No umbrage, no tiredness or fear.
A man in the next room is dreaming in a chair.

THE NINETEENTH-CENTURY NOVEL II

I am the heroine
in a novel, and there are twenty pages left.
Someone is reading the novel, holding
the numbered pages in their hands, almost finished.
Every night, in bed, they read my story
with the novel propped on their chest.
I want them to read quickly, but they read
a page a night, without
urgency, as if there is no rush
before turning off the light.

COME CLOSE

1

The river may not seem deep tilting
over black stones, rippling October.

Beneath there is a pulling, invisible tug
of a forgotten city. *Your body is so soft.*

He said it twice, and twice
he touched me, the way rain

enters a river, disappearing
as if no remnant of him would remain.

2

The sharp blast sunk

into the planet's center when the world was made.

Now a tense wave shakes beneath the land
you walk on.

I will be satisfied

If you feel
            its heat when you

come close.

3

Yesterday I watched a man kneel
over lavender, his hand shaping
the soil for the begonia between his knees.

Daughter and father walk across
the Brooklyn Bridge. He picks her up because she
stumbles. Now she sleeps,
her head heavy against his shoulder.

This morning I woke to men
drilling into the street,
grease on the backs of their necks and arms.
I am tired of fighting. I don't want to argue.

MODESTY

Does the head covering open
the interior eye?

★

The painter conceals the color—Eve emerging
from the hidden
part of Adam—behind black paint.

★

The willow, down-turned and silent, incites
the windows with its long leaves.

★

The clothed body as knowledge.

★

When love is gone
sexual pleasure detaches from the mouth
of the world.

★

The subway heaved forward

and the hand of the man I was with
jerked, from the quick motion, fell
to my waist

for less than one second lightly he touched
me as we lurched, our swoons lit

each tight light to a rupture
into the world beside this one.

★

The Torah is the body we clothe
and its laws are the body we hold
wrapping the soul
folding the soul of souls.

★

How is this longing a longing
for the one who clothes the naked? There is no
romance.

★

What I don't speak you will know.

★

Is the hidden more blessed than the revealed?

★

Why is the holy ark covered? As a woman
covers her body forever flowing and drawn.
When the eye sees inside the ark
God's presence is forgotten
when love is gone.

A GATE WE MIGHT ENTER

The greatest crisis contains a seed.

The seed is a door. Every day

the key clicks
and taps just above, just below the keyhole.

> ★

The door is invisible, the door is oak.
I stand with my back against it.

I knock, my knuckles numb they pass through
the grain, aching they retreat.

The backs of my hands brush against the door,
the memory of a kiss.

I press my cheeks against the cool slab.

The door is wet, my legs frozen fire.

On the other side lies a field, a yellow
living room, a single poppy, last night's sweaty dream.

> ★

Every crisis emits seeds
as when a poppy unwraps in a windy field.

The seeds are gifts, openings into risk.

The seeds are doors. Every day
my hands push against the knotted wood.

IV

WILD

How can a woman find her own wildness?
Where is it? What is woman? Non-man?
Soft dress, long braided hair, non-football, non-president?

The rabbi says to me: "You be the wild one."
"What is wild?" I ask.

I am Robin Hood's bride, deficient until
he leads me through woods, through worlds.
My hand holds the jeweled box, trembling.
How can I reach my own darkness?
How to be a woman? What is woman?

What is a wild woman? If you shave
your head, are you wild? Is rebellion wild?
What does it mean to be fearless?
Are tattoos wild? Being a senator? A poet?
Who is wild? Is she wild? What about
her? Or her? Women poets grow their hair
long down their backs....

When Cleopatra exclaims, "O happy horse to bear
the weight of Antony," she imagines
his fierceness, and she
an actual part of him; he leads,
and the metal bit is under her tongue, she gets
to witness the blood, the jagged terrain.

Rapunzel closes her ebony eyes.
Her couch is gold.
Stretched out in her white gown,
she is a pirate watching herself from the rocky moor.

A dark hums in her throat. Hush.

She dreams a voice: "You be wild."

Danger is opening the fields
of her mind.
A current is undone.

A bare-backed mare canters
over the herbed graves of her parents.

The enchantress, wrinkled, heavy, has locked
Rapunzel in the tower where tall, orange stalks grow,
each with its own artificial glint.

When she wakes, slants of light
and a glass of water. The enormous
synthetic flowers seem to laugh, and she
sings, laughing back at them.

The glass is cold in her hands, fused
and pure like the first thought.
Water blowing clean down her throat.
Slices of light mark the room, wink
off each simulated flower and spangled stem.
She blinks once.

Enchanting the rafters, her thoughts are weird
synthetic wisteria, twisting in cracks and corners.

Her hair shakes,
the ceiling fan catches her dream in its net.

Is this a breach into a wild sanity? With the tips
of her fingers she touches the sparkly plant:

she is an orange vine stretching, her voiceprints
stream down the ivied wall
toward the heath.

THOUGH I DON'T SEE YOU

Spaces between cricket sounds   between
fireflies   flashlight

Even between the bomb and the screams
after the bomb   before
the screams

The broken ground   a tangle of roots

In books   the hair piled on Isabel Archer's head
wrinkles of Gatsby's small palm
the cracks in Huck's raft when he decides
he will go to hell

Something invisible in the body
and in the poem   unspoken
untasted   unsmelled

the man in the late
restaurant who reads
the newpaper   the growing
triangular space between his arm and belly
as he lifts his tired arm

the day's silences
after someone stops laughing or the moment

previous to laughter's beginning   before
the waiter moves his lips   when the pigeon's
wing is about to lift
not when the destination is known   just before knowledge

Before pain started   and when
the pain began
After the nails spewed
from the bomb   when they entered
during

THE RABBI SPEAKS OF *COMFORT* AT THE SHIVA FOR HIS FATHER

"When my father was in the coma
there was life there   I am telling you

life was happening   I still
had a father....   Now

what is *comfort*?

When someone says, 'He lived a full life,' is that *comfort*?"

★

A sitting house in a thicket
of brownish snow

Winter people

Snow   often bridal

today
funereal   plaintive

★

"But what is *comfort*?
Is it, 'He completed his potential'?"

★

Faces floating through hallway
bedroom   kitchen   The rabbi   his black torn
shirt   torn face eyes   sitting on kitchen tiles

"Is it, 'He is still alive in memory'?"

★

A sitting house in a thicket
of brownish snow

Winter people

Snow   often bridal

★

The rabbi speaks of another comfort
circulating the laws

over physics of snow   the other
reality soaking

into the children's footsteps

We asked the question
already not believing

the answer: "Rabbi... Do you believe
you'll see your father again?"

PRAYER MOUTH, NEW YORK CITY

When I wake: a tumbling

like stones in a dryer. I pick myself up,
stare into the colors

of my room, drenched in dreams I can't remember
or don't want to.

Building
is now *shriek.*
The word *body,*
shroud.

Smoke across the river.
In the river. In windows.
(In people?)

Did what happened
happen?

Waking into the tumbling, into the buckling.
The electric animals are standing

on their hind legs in the mains, sobbing,
walking like humans
through the marl and shale under the tremulous city.

WHO RELEASES THE BOUND, WHO STRAIGHTENS THE BENT

Underneath this missing another
missing: familiar, unremembered. The mirror

stares at my bed, the bookshelves have nothing
to say to me. This longing

hangs heavy, the taste of it
filling the back of my mouth. Black rain
suspends past shut windows and brick.

A breathing in my dress
when I bend to the drawer for a shirt,

when air slides through the slit
under the unopened window and reaches my naked elbow.

Let the longing lift north attaching
to the next rung and the next until I speak

translucent, seeable
give me quick
transparent noticing, close.

What is real?
Thin bones glow
in my ankle, my rib,

a hand rests above the roof
of my house,

above the oak beside it.
Blessed are you who releases the bound.

Ache in my unwinged thighs, my belly an unblessed field.
Who straightens the bent
over. Your many names are stuck in my throat.

JERUSALEM III

Sometimes the broom is brittle; or it's a damp
nest, useless.

Let's praise
even those who, for now, lean
on the hinge

resisting the parts of love that bring
only peace.

Blessed are you who girds us with strength.

Evening: splinters of fret strike these stone roads
wet.

In this rough country, in the rough
morning light
night rain fills the broom.

THE VESSEL

The drawbridge splits.
A vessel, abundant

with rough sunburnt faces upturned
with rough sunburnt paint-chipped deck and hull
passes north.

The past—a wave of saffron—murmurs
flung among winter trees.

Yes, grief happened, will happen.
What's left
from the harvest: green husks, a transparent shell, crust.

The drawbridge unlocks, allows
a narrow passage,
the vessel winks at the city, passes north of memory.

NORTH OF MEMORY

I was pressing against the north's saffron star
and it would not listen, hidden
it kept not paying heed kept

disregarding my sharpness, my ragged requests and talk,
then once the north pressed back pushing me back

I softened into dream: *I'll turn silence with my hip.*

In the morning, a dance. My hip touching
memory, I drop
my handkerchief on the synagogue floor.

★

Memory converts
into my friend's e-mail message about her baby:

She keeps breathing the same even breaths,
each breath the same as the one before,
her breaths are steady are equal.

★

Smoke spirals from mute pages, the books
on my shelves gasping from the flames.
Thomas Hardy: "Break me, make me new."

Memory burning through the plywood, Anne Brontë unknots
from the glued spine;

George Eliot: "Admit me, go north, unprison
my male hands."
Blessed are you who did not make me a slave.

★

Go north from the memory of a shrouded word—*schiz-*
ophrenia—heard, but not understood.

When the father's words cut and snapped
wood—go north from the sweet

rotting love draining marrow to the bone, leave
it in all its banal splendor.

Then Lizzy's fish arrived from Alaska tastes flawed, taken
raw wronged from broken wet ice complete.
Thank you for making me according to your will.

★

Sometimes I find that I am as in a field a silken tent
held down by silver stakes wrapped

in spots of clinging mud, the fabric billowing
then taut, then lifting, the ropes relent, slack then firm,

at ease, the winter slants its light through laws, shadows,
through cords loosely bound by silken ties,

the central cedar pole shoots north.
I am all airy silken bondage.

Blessed are you for not making me be
from one of the other nations.

★

I am building my room.
Buried April bells.

74

Kicking off shoes, eyes
closed in a blue bed.

Who removes sleep
from my eyes...

Hushed ringing in my belly, open
into water, swim up

and kiss. Breakfast table.
Leaves splash against windows.

Gray seeps in. Bureau with mirror, boxes,
bracelets and sticks.

Water is in the ceiling.
Rocks are in the floor.

Rain is in my eyes.
The kitchen is cooking rice.

★

There's a new sound in the cold trees, delicate,
deliberate

soon water will run down the jagged bark.

Just give me a simple happiness
with a distance sharer. Books
on a breakfast table, crumpled napkins.

Raw winds tear through the highest branches:
futile the winds to a heart in port.

Lamp and chair. The inverse of the crumbled house.

★

The camel stumbles into the chicken's house, Ha! breaks the roof: squawking, feathers, a beak, a wing; fumbling into a new funny life.

POEM

My urban, my illicit drawers, my mollusk.

My Phileas Fogg buying me Chinese silk.

Darcy and Mr. Rochester, Shanghai brown eyes,
my dashing rabbi, my compass.

My invisible man.

My partner in a French farce.
My partner in a Greek Day parade.

Radish-eater, my swashbuckler,
my Chabad House.

My teffilin-splendor.

Mezuzah-kisser, horse-bettor, my Peanuts
comic strip, my LAX.

My climber of Romanian
mountains, of the Great Wall of China.

My zest, dozer rolled
or stretched on the couch. My nineteenth-century novel.

Sleepy-time bear, my modest, my Professor Bhaer.

Unchildhood, my north, unfather,
my east, my Jerusalem stone.

Dozing chip, my spark-plug
and snippets, my door, my open.

AFTERWARD, EVE

I can't remember
what this brush between my legs is for.
I used to know. And the purpose
of these breasts, of this
tongue, this palm.
It had something to do with.
Now I want.

NOTES

"Unhappiness on Earth": Several lines are from letters of John Keats.

"Seduction": Owes something to the lectures of Dr. Avivah Gottlieb Zornberg.

"Think of This": Several lines in the third section are from *Daniel Deronda* by George Eliot.

"Desire": Owes something to the lectures of Dr. Avivah Gottlieb Zornberg.

"A Gate We Might Enter": The title is from a phrase in a line of Jane Kenyon's poem "Things."

"Wild": This poem owes a debt to the sculptures of JoAnne Carson. The word "voiceprint" is lifted from June Jordan.

"Modesty": Several phrases are from Elizabeth Bishop's "At the Fishhouses."

"Though I Don't See You": The title is from a line from "Shir Hacavode" (Song of Glory), attributed to Rabbi Yehuda HaChassid, the twelfth-century scholar and Kabbalist.

"North of Memory": The title comes from a dream of Diana Miller's, and this poem is for her. The fifth section owes a debt to Robert Frost's "The Silken Tent." The phrase "distance sharer," from Jean Valentine's poem "Night Porch," appears in the seventh section, and a line from Emily Dickinson's "Wild Nights" appears in the same section.

ABOUT THE AUTHOR

Eve Grubin was born and raised in New York City. Her poems have been published in *The American Poetry Review, Barrow Street, LIT, The New Republic, Pleiades, Pool, The Virginia Quarterly Review*, and elsewhere. A chapbook-size group of poems appeared in *Conjunctions* (Fall 2004) with an afterword by Fanny Howe. She has been a Yaddo fellow, and holds degrees from Smith College (B.A.), Sarah Lawrence College (M.F.A.), and Middlebury College's Bread Loaf School of English (M.A.). She works as the programs director at the Poetry Society of America, and she teaches poetry at The New School University. A doctoral candidate in English at CUNY's Graduate Center, she is the poetry editor at *Lyric* and a fellow at The Drisha Institute for Jewish Education.